Autumn Allure

A Seasonal Collection of Pin-Ups and Fashion Illustrations

Foreword

Images of beautiful women, fashionably dressed (or not at all) have been around for a very long time. The rise of the golden age of illustration at the end of the nineteenth and beginning of the twentieth centuries led to the era of the "Pin-Up", a charming young woman, beautifully dressed (or mostly undressed) in a particular situation, often cute or humorous.

Artists such as Gil Elvgren, Joyce Ballantyne, Alberto Vargas, and Earl Moran perfected the art form, which fell out of fashion in the 1960s, for various reasons.

Some of these images were quite spicy, verging on "nudie" or even erotica, but many were mild, not much more explicit than a standard advertising illustration.

We have chosen to go with the mild approach in these illustrations, with an emphasis on vintage-style charm. They are also printed on only one side of the page, so there is no bleed through, and the images may be removed from the book if desired, to be used as prints, etc.

Enjoy this collection of Autumnal beauties!

Happy Fall!